by W.T. Kosmos

A one-act comedy featuring six or more actors, minimal props, and a satirical exploration of unwavering loyalty to authoritarian leaders, intolerance, and environmental mayhem. After the monarchy falls, the Lumberjack Leprechauns hold a costume contest to find their next golden leader. For teens and adults.

WISEWIT
PRESS

Wise Wit Press, LLC

The Golden One
A Comedy

Copyright © 2024 by W.T. Kosmos

Summary: A one-act comedy featuring six or more actors, minimal props, and a satirical exploration of unwavering loyalty to authoritarian leaders, intolerance, and environmental mayhem. After the monarchy falls, the Lumberjack Leprechauns hold a costume contest to find their next golden leader. For teens and adults.

ISBN paperback 979-8-9883151-6-2

ISBN e-book 979-8-9883151 7-9

CHARACTERS

JUDGES *(Lumberjack Leprechauns)*
SAWDUNCE
CHOPWIT
AXESTORM

TALENT TOTER
BLARNEY

CANDIDATES *(in order of appearance)*
PIG
NURSE
OWL
PRESIDENT LEAFHOPPER
BODYGUARD
SHEEP
SHEEP'S MOM
WILLOW
GUIDE
THUMPER
KING

Preface

In an era of division, intolerance, and social issues that pressure test the foundations of democracy and the sustainability of our planet, one day, weeks away from Halloween, two hilarious ideas popped into my head. The first was a skit for Saturday Night Live featuring failed castle rioters choosing a new leader with a costume contest. The second was that Saturday Night Live might actually produce it. I did some research, recognized my silliness, and decided to do something more ludicrous: write a play instead. And thanks to rounds of feedback from theatre friends, I can't wait to see who produces it.

This one-act show—that exposes ecological absurdities and lampoons loyalty to authoritarian leaders—is, of course, designed for school, college, or community spaces that still allow theatre, the arts, and thinking. However, this satire with minimal props is a barrel of fun for virtually any occasion. For example, at parties, Halloween gatherings, table readings with the in-laws, teen sleepovers, the half-time show of the Super Bowl, heads of state inaugurations, and so on.

If you perform this play, I do not know how your audience will respond. However, like democracy, audience participation is strongly encouraged. And while certainty is often the great rallying cry of whackadoodles, one thing is sure: no live performance will ever be the same.

Spoons up!

W.T. Kosmos
Humorist Author and Playwright
Paradox, USA, Earth, Milky Way

Directing Notes

- The characters can be played by any gender. Thus, pronoun text may be changed.
- How to construct the door is an important choice (cardboard, solid oak, etc.), which will have different comedic effects. Likewise with the choice of axes, spoons, and spoon helmets (large or small, real, plastic, etc.).
- Please take time to anticipate and know your audience. Consult with your medical, legal, and security teams as necessary.

W.T. Kosmos

To the curious and courageous truth seekers.

At a discreet location in the North Woods, three Lumberjack Leprechauns sit at a judge's table in a cabin stewing over an unsuccessful day of finding their next leader. SAWDUNCE has bandages wrapped around his arms and hands.

CHOPWIT: This method for finding The Golden One isn't working! We haven't found a single decent contestant!

AXESTORM: It's going to work! There's just a labor shortage right now.

SAWDUNCE: (*tugging at bandages*) What's our highest rated contestant so far?

CHOPWIT: (*shuffling through papers*) Eight total points. No, wait. Nine. No one has even reached double digits and qualified for the leader board. Great Mother of Gold—are these contestants even qualified? Wait, do we have qualifications?

AXESTORM: Chopwit, we already discussed this! The Golden One will lead a storming of the castle, oust the new "president", release our captured leader Stumpsharp, end this ridiculous democracy, and restore the monarchy. Then, once again, we can chop down all the trees we want and finally find the long-lost buried great pot o' gold!

CHOPWIT: Maybe it's the flyer.

AXESTORM: The flyer is fine! (*grabs flyer and reads*)
Seeking The Golden One
Become the next leader of the Lumberjack Leprechauns!
Contestants will:
- demonstrate leadership talent for storming the castle and restoring the monarchy
- model a clever costume best suited for storming

the castle

The winner will also win a golden prize!

Find us at a secret location in the North Woods!

CHOPWIT: It does seem clear.

AXESTORM: Yes. We need a leader who is clever, cunning, and courageous. And our flyer and process for finding such a talented leader is an ingenious way to do just that!

CHOPWIT: We'll see. But I think The Golden One should have a sense of humor, too.

AXESTORM: Humor won't help us storm the castle!

CHOPWIT: It would help leprechaun morale, which isn't exactly sky-high right now.

AXESTORM: Chopwit, this isn't the time for giggles and games.

SAWDUNCE: Did you bring games? I love games!

AXESTORM: We don't have time for giggles and games!

CHOPWIT: Maybe democracy could work if each leprechaun counted as two votes.

AXESTORM: Democracy will never work!

SAWDUNCE: So, we're going to oust President Leafhopper?

AXESTORM: Sawdunce, do not ever say that name again.

CHOPWIT: Long live the king!

AXESTORM: Long live the king!

SAWDUNCE: Huh? The king lost the election and ran away with a pot o' gold. Is he still the king?

AXESTORM: Yes!

CHOPWIT: Well, unofficially the king, until the monarchy is restored.

AXESTORM: Ahh! And the king didn't run away— the king is *hiding* until The Golden One restores the monarchy. That's why we tried to storm the castle! And do I need to remind you that the king pays us to chop down trees?

CHOPWIT: It would be nice if the king gave us a raise for once. Have you seen the cost of a new axe?

AXESTORM: Forget the raise. The king can't pay us anything now.

SAWDUNCE: Oh! So, if we find the great pot o' gold —

AXESTORM: *When* we find the great pot o' gold.

SAWDUNCE: When we find the great pot o' gold, we won't need to give the king half of it, because he's no longer the king!

AXESTORM: As usual, you're missing something.

SAWDUNCE: Oh, right. I'll miss the royal parades. I love when leprechauns gather together. But parades would be better if they handed out something to eat—

AXESTORM: No, Sawdunce, that's not what you're missing. If we want to find the gold, we need unlimited tree chopping, and if we want that, then we must restore the monarchy by storming the castle. But if parades are what motivates you—

SAWDUNCE: Wait. Was Stumpsharp The Golden One?

AXESTORM: No. Do you ever listen? Sadly, Stumpsharp did not reach that level, despite the ingenious success of using stilts to cross the moat. He broke his limbs bravely scaling the castle wall, which as you know, was a very long fall, especially for us who are not so tall. Without functional arms to cut wood, he can no longer be our fearless leader. The king said that Stumpsharp would be dubbed the Bronze One, or perhaps, the Pewter One once the monarchy is restored. Regardless, The Golden One we select today will not only lead the Lumberjack Leprechauns, The Golden One will save the king and save the country!

SAWDUNCE: Exciting!

AXESTORM: Today is beyond exciting. It's momentous, historic. It carries the weight of a triple rainbow.

SAWDUNCE: Whoa. Heavy.

AXESTORM: Perhaps if we attacked the castle at night.

SAWDUNCE: Scary!

CHOPWIT: Regardless of *when* we attack, we need much taller stilts. How many leprechauns did we lose crossing the moat? And those stilts were terrible for climbing castle walls!

SAWDUNCE: Yeah! When I fell, I scraped me wee hands and arms!

CHOPWIT: Many did. Thus, the need for very tall stilts that can reach the top of the castle walls, or at least, allow us to peek over. Or, maybe, we need a new plan.

AXESTORM: We need a new leader!

SAWDUNCE: Maybe this cabin is too hard to find.

CHOPWIT: (*peers out the window*) So cloudy today. Perhaps we should have provided directions.

AXESTORM: No! That's part of the leadership test! How can someone lead *us* if they get lost in the woods?

SAWDUNCE: But why this spooky place?

AXESTORM: So the leafnuts won't find us! And those Tree Huggers are too terrified to enter the North Woods. Imagine if either knew about our secret mission. (*to Sawdunce*) And you're a Lumberjack Leprechaun—how can you be afraid of the woods?!

SAWDUNCE: This seems like a forest to me. These trees are tall. Imagine if one fell on me. And there aren't any leprechauns here.

AXESTORM: That's the point! That's why the leafnuts and Tree Huggers can't find us.

SAWDUNCE: What is the point of all of this? You know, everything that happened when we stormed the castle—Stumpsharp's broken limbs, the friends we lost in the moat, not to mention me scraped arms and hands—have stirred so many questions deep in me soul. What is the point of me life?

AXESTORM: This is not the time to question our mission!

BLARNEY: (*knocks on the door, enters*)

AXESTORM: Blarney, how many times have we been over this? The protocol is that you announce the contestant, and then, and only then, will I grant you permission to enter.

BLARNEY: Lighten up, Axestorm. I was peeing in the woods. Sorry, no contestant.

AXESTORM: You may enter, talent toter.

BLARNEY: How does this place not have a loo? So, as I was out there, thinking, like I do, it only makes sense that I should get a vote, too.

CHOPWIT: Decent rhyming, but not a limerick.

AXESTORM: No voting for you.

SAWDUNCE: You're one quarter Tree Hugger.

BLARNEY: There's no evidence of that!

CHOPWIT: You climbed a giant oak.

BLARNEY: Did you see the size of that tree—it was magnificent! And at the top, you could see far, far away to exotic lands that I will visit someday—I mean, I was up there seeing which branches to cut before the trunk.

AXESTORM: Rookie.

CHOPWIT: How convenient that your birth certificate was ruined in the moat.

BLARNEY: Stupid uneven stilts. Just let me vote—there's a lot riding on today's selection of The Golden One!

AXESTORM: The king said no.

BLARNEY: But I can cut down a tree twice as fast as ol' two left hands Sawdunce, whose hands are also scraped now in case you didn't notice.

CHOPWIT: Doesn't matter.

SAWDUNCE: Liar! I have a right hand.

CHOPWIT: (*turns to Blarney*) You know the rules. We rate each contestant, select the top five, and then the three of us—the true Lumberjack Leprechauns—must reach consensus for choosing our new leader, AKA, The Golden One.

AXESTORM: Do we have a problem, talent toter?

BLARNEY: No, no we don't. (*turns to audience, secretly*) We don't have a problem because these three buffoons are easily persuaded with audience flattery. I'll bet you hate when people take your power away. Can you help me choose the next leader of the Lumberjack Leprechauns? (*exits*)

PIG is outside the door, oinking.

BLARNEY: (*pounds on the door*) Our next contestant is dressed as a Pig.

AXESTORM: You may enter, talent toter.

BLARNEY: (*returns with PIG who continues oinking.*

BLARNEY *walks through the door, waving his hand from the stench. He turns to the audience.*) I need a new job.

PIG: (*Rushes over to the refreshment stand, stuffs his face with food, slogs down brew, making a mess. Wads up cup, throws it in the trash, faces the judges*) How was that for an entrance?

SAWDUNCE: Is he a real pig?

AXESTORM: (*to the other judges, waving away a foul smell*) Have we seen enough—

PIG: Wow! Who made the brew?

CHOPWIT: That is my lucky golden brew.

PIG: You should let me sell that for you. I'll give you 50% of the profits. No? Keep thinking about it. I might give you 60%. Sorry about the smell. I slipped and rolled in something nasty a few minutes ago. More importantly, I can't believe what our new "leader" leaf nutty nut nut has taken away from hard-working Lumberjack Leprechauns.

CHOPWIT: What now?!

AXESTORM: (*stands up*) Don't mess with us Pig!

PIG: Whoa. Calm down, I'm just the hungry messenger. Actually, name's Jack Ham, AKA, the king's, uh, I mean, the former king's Super Golden Land Developer and Real Estate Mogul. Now I work independently. (*hands out business cards, JUDGES wave away the smell*) Your team has done a marvelous job clearing land, I mean, chopping trees. Oh, can you believe all these new regulations? Now school is required for kids, which means they can't work for me. Now you can only cut down four trees per day, which means less land to develop and fewer straw houses I can sell. We have mutual interests, if you know what I mean.

SAWDUNCE: I've been living under a rock. Straw houses are itchy.

BLARNEY: Hey, are you the one who sold my cousin that straw shack that blew away?

CHOPWIT: Never mind these two. Finding the buried great pot o' gold was already hard enough! Now it's four trees per day?! Per lumberjack? Or per team?

PIG: Not sure. Did you say something about a buried pot o' gold?

SAWDUNCE: Yeah, we've been looking forever! We chop down trees. Then we have to shovel the dirt and pickaxe the roots. Now me wee hands are scraped and blistered!

AXESTORM: (*to the other judges*) Both of you, shut up! That's not public knowledge.

PIG: Ah, the king is more cunning than I realized— I mean, what a noble endeavor!

SAWDUNCE: After I scraped me wee hands on the castle wall, I have so many questions.

AXESTORM: (*slaps his head*) Sawdunce here has lost his wee mind. Listen, we're running out of time. You got a plan to storm the castle or what?

PIG: Of course I have a plan! We disguise ourselves as starving pigs, like me. Those animal-loving leafnuts will open the castle door to feed us!

CHOPWIT: Maybe. But as stupid as they are, they'll recognize we aren't real pigs as we get closer. What else you got?

PIG: I've got a herd of fast ponies that can stampede through the castle and over President Leafhopper ——

AXESTORM: Don't say that name!

PIG: And they can plow land faster than you can drink

a shamrock shake. We'll find your lost pot o' gold in no time!

AXESTORM: I guess the gold's out of the pot.

CHOPWIT: What kind of ponies?

PIG: Standard.

CHOPWIT: So, not magical or flying ones. All standard size?

PIG: Yes. Well, maybe a few miniature ones.

SAWDUNCE: Plows would break the pot!

CHOPWIT: Sawdunce has a point for once.

PIG: Oh, no. Remember, I said ponies. Not horses.

SAWDUNCE: Horses?! (*dives under table*)

PIG: And my ponies are one of a kind! They can plow land, storm castles, and find lost gold.

AXESTORM: Amazing! But what's your share? I mean, if your ponies happened to dig up the pot o' gold?

PIG: Ah, with your amazing lumberjack skills, and my ponies, I'll let you keep all the gold. And I'll just take the land.

AXESTORM: Astonishing.

CHOPWIT: It seems too good to be true.

SAWDUNCE: (*returns to seat*) Yeah, how do we know we can trust you?

PIG: You know who wants to regulate straw houses? President Leafhopper!

AXESTORM: Don't say that name! He has rules for straw houses now, too? This is vital information. You are an excellent contestant. Let's rate already! Stick around Pig. There's hope for you to be our next leader!

PIG rushes to the refreshment table, throws remaining snacks and jugs of brew into a bag.

BLARNEY: (*escorts PIG outside, returns*)

CHOPWIT: Any additional discussion, or are we ready to rate?

AXESTORM: This is our first clever plan! We dress as starving pigs. When the leafnuts lower the drawbridge, we charge with ponies and storm the castle. And what a bonus—his ponies can plow land much faster than we can pickaxe it. Finally, we will fulfill our destiny! Now, let's rate! (*Holds up a number 9*)

BLARNEY: I don't like this guy. Smells a little shady. (*appeals to the audience to boo*)

AXESTORM: Perhaps one less point for the smell. (*Holds up a number 8*)

SAWDUNCE: (*gives a 6 rating*) I had a bad experience with a pony as a wee lad.

CHOPWIT: Miniature pony?

SAWDUNCE: Regular.

CHOPWIT: Sorry. (*gives a 5 rating, writing down the results*) Well, I would have discussed this with the whole group, you know, to be a team player, but the first rating was already cast. (*glares at Axestorm*) I have no problems with dressing up as pigs or using ponies that can plow, but without magical flying powers how are the ponies going to gallop across the drawbridge and through the entrance before they realize we aren't real pigs? And I doubt those ponies can swim across the moat with us riding on their backs. And even if they could, what's the point if the castle door is closed? Well, that makes a score of 19. (*writes on the results board*)

SAWDUNCE: A solid first place.

AXESTORM: Soon, there will be more contestants on

that leader board! Pig just needs to stay in the top five. Then we will reach consensus for the next leader of the Lumberjack Leprechauns!

NURSE: (*knocks on the door*) Hello? Anyone in there? I'm very thirsty!

NURSE is wearing a nurse's cap with a red cross emblem. She is wrapped in mismatched, heavy winter gear layers including a thick coat, a thin coat, scarf, and gloves. Outside her thick coat is a giant, over-sized stethoscope. Underneath winter gear, she is wearing mismatched scrubs, perhaps with stripes and polka dots, and mismatching medical gloves, one short, one long. Bright neon band-aids and bright neon bandage tape are concealed in her inner layer pockets.

AXESTORM: (*waves his arms wildly at BLARNEY to do his job*)

BLARNEY: Get the next contestant. Chop wood. Carry water. Get the next contestant. Chop wood. Carry water—

AXESTORM: Blarney! You aren't chopping wood or carrying water today.

BLARNEY: Get the next contestant. Chop wood. Carry water. Is this it? Isn't there more to life than working for the king? What about traveling the world? What about love?

AXESTORM: You can find all the love you want after we find the great pot o' gold!

BLARNEY: (*exits and shuts the door. Moments later, pounds on the door excitedly*) Our next contestant is dressed as a Nurse.

AXESTORM: You may enter, talent toter.

BLARNEY: (*enters with NURSE*) This might be the one! (*appeals to audience*)

NURSE: (*sweating, exhausted*) What good fortune. I really needed to get away and wham! A flyer for a costume contest shows up. But what a hike. And warmer than I expected! Wow, am I thirsty! (*panting, scans the judges and room. Judges exchange confused glances.*) And apparently I'm talking to myself. Well, your costumes are hilarious, but where is everyone? I thought this was a party. So much for finding my soul mate.

AXESTORM: This is a contest to determine the leader of the Lumberjack Leprechauns.

NURSE: Right. Well, lucky you, I dressed up as a nurse.

SAWDUNCE: You're sweating. Are you hot?

NURSE: Thank you for noticing. Now if someone could—

CHOPWIT: Clearly, she's hot.

BLARNEY: (*smitten*) You have my temperature rising.

NURSE: Oh, I see. Am I a *hot* nurse? As opposed to a nurse who takes care of people and gives and gives and gives, every day and every night for years on end, without receiving anything in return, not even a simple thank you. Obviously, the universe is trying to tell me something. What am I doing wrong? It doesn't matter how far I go, or how I dress, I can't escape pigs.

SAWDUNCE: No, the pig left. We're leprechauns!

NURSE: Right, right. Of course you are. And let me guess—you are searching for a great pot o' gold?

AXESTORM: How did you know that?!

NURSE: Okay, I can respect staying in character... But seriously, good grief, what is the temperature in here? I'm dying. (*tosses off gloves, lassos BLARNEY with a scarf, pulling him in close*) So thirsty!

BLARNEY: I've been thirsty for a long time, too.

NURSE: If only I had something to drink. (*tosses scarf to the side*)

BLARNEY: I wonder who could quench your thirst?

CHOPWIT: Enough of this foolishness! Your costume is interesting. But how is it suited for storming the castle? And why should we select you as our next leader?

NURSE: Ah... you are the judges. (*approaches SAWDUNCE*) Oh no. Your head has a little boo boo. (*pulls band-aid from pocket and places it on SAWDUNCE's forehead*) And, oh my—your poor hands! Let me help you. (*pulls tape from pocket and wraps bandage poorly. NURSE uses a stethoscope to check SAWDUNCE's heartbeat*). Thank goodness your heart is strong. I think you'll survive. (*Beat*) What, no applause for that performance—did you see how I stayed in character?

BLARNEY: (*clapping wildly*) Marvelous!

SAWDUNCE: My bandage is a bit tight.

AXESTORM: How will you storm the castle?!

NURSE: You want to know how this hot nurse will storm the castle? Play some music and I'll show you! (*CHOPWIT shrugs, plays upbeat music. NURSE dances with clumsy, exaggerated moves*) I'm so hot. So hot! (*sweating with rising irritation, tosses thick coat at Blarney*)

BLARNEY: (*misreads the signal and waves the coat wildly to whip up the crowd*) Let's go!

NURSE: I'm roasting like a shamrock on a sunny day! (*sheds and throws thin coat at CHOPWIT*) I'm sizzling like a boiled potato! (*now in scrubs, NURSE whips her nurse's cap at BLARNEY, then she grabs and puts on AXESTORM'S hat*) I'm so hot, I could fry an egg on me wee hat!

AXESTORM folds his arms. CHOPWIT and SAWDUNCE begin dancing. BLARNEY appeals to the audience to cheer.

NURSE: I'm so scorching, even me lucky charms are sweating! So thirsty. If only someone could quench my thirst (*grabs BLARNEY*) Seriously, I AM REALLY HOT! You got anything to drink around here?!

BLARNEY: Oh. Oh! (*glances at his mug of brew, reluctant to share*)

CHOPWIT: Sorry, our previous contestant took all the snacks.

NURSE: Another pig. So, you don't have anything to drink?

BLARNEY: (*grabs mug*) Here—I saved some brew.

NURSE: (*continues dancing*) Thank you. Finally, someone taking care of me for once! (*chugs brew*) Wow. (*shakes BLARNEY, then kisses him. BLARNEY swoons.*) So good! Delicious! What is that?

CHOPWIT: It's a batch of me lucky golden brew. You like it?

NURSE (*desperate, drinks more*) Love it. But… you're already out of drink and food? Where is everyone? Is this really it?

CHOPWIT: We're on a tight budget—we put most of our resources into storming the castle.

NURSE: Great party.

AXESTORM: Cut the music! Although you are a talented dancer, how will you lead us in storming the castle? I don't see how your costume will help us accomplish our mission. None of your performance makes sense!

NURSE: You are really committed to staying in character! Remind me: What do I get if I win this contest? You know, if I become the leader of the Lumberjack Leprechauns?

CHOPWIT: You'll share a great pot o' gold.

NURSE: Of course.

CHOPWIT: And a lifetime supply of my lucky golden brew?

NURSE: (*suddenly excited, dances*) Well, now we're talking. And lucky for you—we don't need to storm the castle. Winter gear will confuse the castle people.

AXESTORM: You mean the leafnuts.

NURSE: They sound fun.

AXESTORM: How can you not know who lives— You know that we had an election, right?

NURSE: What's an election?

AXESTORM: You didn't vote?!

NURSE: Vote? We have a king.

CHOPWIT: Wow.

AXESTORM: Anyway… How will your costume help us storm the castle?

NURSE: In case you didn't notice, my dancing is contagious. Dressed like nurses in winter gear, we'll dance our way straight in! (*dances with exaggerated, clumsy moves*)

CHOPWIT: That's a long shot.

AXESTORM: Preposterous!

SAWDUNCE: I think it could work.

AXESTORM: Where you are from?

NURSE: The big city.

CHOPWIT: You traveled all the way from the city?

NURSE: That's right. I needed a change, and wham! There's a flyer for a costume contest in the North Woods!

CHOPWIT: You already said that.

BLARNEY: It's a reminder that everything happens for a reason.

AXESTORM: The city! How can a city twig lead the Lumberjack Leprechauns? Have you even swung an axe?

NURSE: Why would I ever need to do that?

AXESTORM: Who was in charge of marketing?

CHOPWIT: Blarney.

AXESTORM: Blarney!

BLARNEY: I would love to travel to the city. And then around the world.

AXESTORM: You have a job—stay focused!

BLARNEY: And what a wonderful plan to storm the castle! The leafnuts love to dance! They'll lower the drawbridge as we dance our way over the moat, through the door, and into the castle! Wouldn't the Nurse make a lovely leader? (*appeals to the audience. Judges exchange glances, as if persuaded by the crowd's energy*)

CHOPWIT: Thank you, Nurse. We must deliberate in private now. Please stay close by, we will announce the finalists soon. (*motions for the NURSE to leave*)

NURSE grabs and tips mug to capture remaining drops of brew and exits.

CHOPWIT: Any additional discussion, or are we

ready to rate?

AXESTORM: Rate! (*Holds up the number 4*)

BLARNEY: Only a 4? The Nurse contestant deserved
a 10! (*appeals for crowd support*)

SAWDUNCE: At least a 9. (*gives a 9 rating*)

CHOPWIT: (*gives a 7 rating, writing down the results*)
Well, that's our best yet. A total score of 20! (*writes
it on the leader board*)

AXESTORM: The Nurse cannot be The Golden One.

OWL: (*outside the door*) Hoo! Hoo!

BLARNEY: (*rushes out the door, returns confused*) I swore
I heard another contestant. (*OWL "flies" in*)

SAWDUNCE: Ah! Owls eat leprechauns! (*dives under
table*)

CHOPWIT: It's an owl costume you idiot! (*to
BLARNEY*) We have an entrance protocol around
here!

OWL:
With a hoot, the owl did say,

In this festive contest, let's play,

But let's also honor the trees so tall,

For they are the guardians of us all,

And in their wisdom, we find our way.

BLARNEY: What? (*attempts to escort OWL toward the
door*)

CHOPWIT: A limerick! Never mind the entrance. I'll
allow it.

AXESTORM: I don't like contestants who speak in
the third person.

CHOPWIT: Let's cut to the chase. Why are you here
Owl?

OWL:

> The leprechauns, with their pots of gold,
> And the trees, with their leaves so bold,
> Joined by the animals, wild and free,
> Together they danced, in glee,
> For in their union, a story was told.

CHOPWIT: This contestant speaks in limericks. A true ally!

SAWDUNCE: This Owl knows where the buried pot o' gold is! It's a St. Paddy's miracle!

OWL: (*confused, then cheers*) Hoo! Hoo!

AXESTORM: Fools! How could this contestant know where my great, great, great grandfather's pot o' gold is buried? Trees and roots have grown all around it. We've been cutting down trees and searching for generations!

OWL:

> With wisdom vast and vision keen,
> The owl said, Our search must be clean,
> We'll find the gold without harm,
> For the answer lies not in the trees' arm,
> But in the magic that's unseen.

SAWDUNCE: This Owl can help us with its magical powers!

CHOPWIT: It isn't a real Owl.

SAWDUNCE: What about storming the castle, wise Owl?

OWL:

> Imagine the sight, oh what a jest,
> Leprechauns charging, doing their best,
> But alas, the castle's walls were high,
> And your efforts were silly and did go awry,
> Ending in a humorous, chaotic fest.

SAWDUNCE: How did the Owl know what happened? It is a wise Owl. Maybe it's not a costume!

CHOPWIT: Ridiculous. Besides, that could be a disqualification; costumes are required.

AXESTORM: What is your purpose here?

OWL:

> The leprechauns, with their emerald hue,
> And the trees, with their leaves so true,
> With the animals, they shared a dream,
> Together they'd work, as a team,
> And in their collaboration, their world grew.

SAWDUNCE: This Owl wants to build an army of leprechauns and woodland creatures to storm the castle! It's right: We can't do it alone!

CHOPWIT: Clever! And no enemy spy could speak in limericks!

AXESTORM: Good point. Sure, owls could fly into the castle. But what about the other woodland creatures? And what about us?! How will dressing up as owls help us storm the castle?

CHOPWIT: Yes, Owl, how can we work together?

OWL:

> As an owl, I make a plea,
> To you leprechauns, hear my decree,
> Our trees so grand, let's not fell,
> For they're homes where many dwell,
> Let's keep them standing, for all to see.
>
> Each chop you make, each tree you take,
> Brings harm to life, a grave mistake,
> The creatures, the birds, in distress,
> Rely on trees for food and rest,

So let's preserve, for nature's sake.

With heartfelt words, I urge a pause,
To reflect on nature's laws,
In every tree, life does thrive,
Let's keep them standing, keep them alive,
And protect our forests with a noble cause.

SAWDUNCE: That's a lot of words.

CHOPWIT: A three-part limerick. Amazing. But what is it saying?

AXESTORM: This contestant is saying to stop chopping down trees! How are we going to find the buried pot o' gold if we don't chop down the trees? And the Owl just switched to first person, which is very confusing. Wait a minute—are you a leafnut in disguise?! Get this contestant out of here! (*motions to BLARNEY, who escorts the OWL out of the room*)

CHOPWIT: Any discuss—

AXESTORM: Rate the Owl!

CHOPWIT: Got it. (*holds up a 5*) Potential there, but the plan was underdeveloped.

AXESTORM: (*holds up a 1*) Only because there isn't a zero.

SAWDUNCE: (*holds up a 7*) Surprisingly, I liked the Owl.

CHOPWIT: Very well, that brings the Owl's total to 13, which makes the leader board. (*records on top 5 leader board*)

AXESTORM: Outrageous! I know there are better contestants. And I have a lucky feeling about our next one.

BLARNEY: (*gleeful*) I'll check. Oh, look who's still in first place. (*exits*)

PRESIDENT LEAFHOPPER: (*outside the door, knocks loudly twice*) Knock! Knock! (*She is wearing flip flops, shorts, and a sports jacket.*)

AXESTORM: We have a protocol! Who's there?

PRESIDENT LEAFHOPPER: Guess.

AXESTORM: What? We have a protocol around here! (*motions to BLARNEY, who exits*)

SAWDUNCE: No, no. She's doing a knock, knock joke! Start over again! Tell us your knock, knock joke.

CHOPWIT: Finally, someone with a sense of humor!

BLARNEY: (*outside*) Uhhh!

PRESIDENT LEAFHOPPER: Knock, knock.

SAWDUNCE: Who's there?

PRESIDENT LEAFHOPPER: Guess.

SAWDUNCE: Guess who?

PRESIDENT LEAFHOPPER: Guess you'll be surprised to see who's come to win your contest.

BLARNEY: (*pounds on the door*) Our next contestant needs no introduction!

AXESTORM: You may enter, talent toter.

PRESIDENT LEAFHOPPER marches in, with flip flops flapping loudly. She occasionally hops while marching. AXESTORM and CHOPWIT grab their axes.

SAWDUNCE: President Leafhopper!

AXESTORM: Don't say that name!

PRESIDENT LEAFHOPPER: Hey, hey, hey. I thought this was a leadership contest, not a shillelagh smackdown. (*strides over to the refreshment table, frowns at the lack of drinks and food*)

AXESTORM: Why are you here?

PRESIDENT LEAFHOPPER: To win of course.

AXESTORM: Not with my vote! How do you know about shillelaghs?

PRESIDENT LEAFHOPPER: I studied my opponent. And I got 15% of the leprechaun vote.

AXESTORM: Lying leafnut! And these are axes, not shillelaghs.

PRESIDENT LEAFHOPPER: You're right about one, but not the other. 15.4% of leprechauns voted for me. (*glances at refreshment table*) In other surprises, a little light on drinks, eh?

CHOPWIT: A pig drank it all.

PRESIDENT LEAFHOPPER: That good, huh?

SAWDUNCE: (*pulls drink from under the table*) Actually, there's one left. (*brings it to PRESIDENT LEAFHOPPER*)

AXESTORM: Sawdunce!

SAWDUNCE: But she's the pres—

AXESTORM: Don't say that word!

BODYGUARD: (*bursts through the door with his flip flops flapping*) Wait! (*snatches drink from PRESIDENT LEAFHOPPER's hand and tests it*) This concoction is breathtaking. You know what would go great with this? Acorn muffins.

PRESIDENT LEAFHOPPER: (*drinks the rest*) Yes! Delicious. Who made this?

CHOPWIT: I did. Where is your costume?

PRESIDENT LEAFHOPPER: I'm a politician. I don't need a costume. You ever thought about selling this brew? One of my campaign promises is to provide small business loans to—

AXESTORM: Enough of this nonsense! Without a costume you aren't qualified to be our next leader, just like you aren't qualified to lead our country!

PRESIDENT LEAFHOPPER: If you'll just give me a few minutes to share my four-point plan, I will earn your support for my presidency and our new democracy.

AXESTORM: Restore the monarchy! Long live the king!

CHOPWIT: Long live the king!

SAWDUNCE: I thought the king is unofficial now?

AXESTORM: Not for long!

PRESIDENT LEAFHOPPER: You see, democracy is a grand experiment based on some crazy ideas.

SAWDUNCE: I like a little mischief.

AXESTORM: You don't want this kind of crazy.

PRESIDENT LEAFHOPPER: Crazy enough, the king and your tree chopping inspired the creation of our democracy.

SAWDUNCE: What?

PRESIDENT LEAFHOPPER: You didn't know that? You've really upset some people! You cut down all the oaks in Oakville. Now they can't have their acorn festival.

BODYGUARD: Or acorn muffins.

PRESIDENT LEAFHOPPER: And they might rename their village to Sadville.

AXESTORM: King's orders. He didn't like the mayor. And we had a solid lead that the great pot o' gold was buried there.

PRESIDENT LEAFHOPPER: Not solid enough. You cut down so many trees in Leaf City they canceled the great leaf pile jumping contest. Without shade, their cobblestone streets are scorching, and their homes are hotter than blazes. And a strange new smog is causing breathing difficulties.

AXESTORM: Small potatoes.

PRESIDENT LEAFHOPPER: Well, it upset them enough to create the Leaf Party, which as you know, boasts the winning president. Then you cut down the trees in the hills, which caused mudslides. And you know who was more upset than the hill people?

SAWDUNCE: Who?

PRESIDENT LEAFHOPPER: The people who live in the valley. Think about it.

SAWDUNCE: Oh no.

AXESTORM: Fake news—that was the Tree Huggers!

PRESIDENT LEAFHOPPER: C'mon! The Tree Huggers cut down trees?

AXESTORM: I heard it on the Shamrock Spin.

PRESIDENT LEAFHOPPER: Then there were the homes that collapsed along with the banks of the Willow River, the farmers' topsoil that blew away with no tree protection, which, in turn, caused food and brew prices to rise, which, of course, led to the Farmers' Party. And then, of course, there are the Tree Huggers, who are as angry as a king with no crown.

AXESTORM: Fake news. And if you make one more king joke—

PRESIDENT LEAFHOPPER: Call it what you want, but most of these folks voted for me.

SAWDUNCE: So, there are more than two political parties?

PRESIDENT LEAFHOPPER: Yep.

AXESTORM: One. Nothing a leafnut says is true. Two. It doesn't make sense because if we found the gold on their land, I'm sure the king would have given them their fair share!

CHOPWIT: Long live the king!

PRESIDENT LEAFHOPPER: Well, we have a democracy now.

SAWDUNCE: Why would we want a democracy? It's complicated.

PRESIDENT LEAFHOPPER: Democracy is like a wild party where everyone's invited, and nobody has to bow to the brute with the biggest muscles or the clown wearing a fancy crown.

AXESTORM: Watch it!

PRESIDENT LEAFHOPPER: Gone are the days of following rules set by the one with the longest beard or the ogre stomping on leprechauns.

SAWDUNCE: I hate ogres.

PRESIDENT LEAFHOPPER: Instead, we all try to agree on basic rights and rules to make life better for everyone. It's like a party where everyone gets a say, and the government is by the people, for the people, and made up of the people. It's messy, but there's a pot at the end of the rainbow.

SAWDUNCE: There is?

PRESIDENT LEAFHOPPER: Yes. Voting! Where citizens choose their leaders and carve the destiny of their dreams.

AXESTORM: But my candidate lost!

SAWDUNCE: I like parties with lots of people.

CHOPWIT: Democracy is a crazy experiment.

AXESTORM: An experiment sure to fail.

PRESIDENT LEAFHOPPER: Democracy will fail if we can't agree on some basic principles, like free and fair elections, where each citizen's vote counts the same, no matter who you are. So, imagine that the people did elect a leprechaun president, which could happen in a democracy.

AXESTORM: I would be okay with that. Now democracy makes sense.

PRESIDENT LEAFHOPPER: Right. So, if a leprechaun president won, don't you think the Leaf Party, Farmers' Party, Tree Huggers, and other parties should accept the results?

AXESTORM: Of course!

PRESIDENT LEAFHOPPER: Excellent. Then based on principle, you understand why I am the rightful president.

AXESTORM: Bah! You're trying to trick us. But you're comparing rainbows and pots of poop.

PRESIDENT LEAFHOPPER: Uhh. You're the one comparing two very different things.

AXESTORM: Exactly! I know that Lumberjack Leprechauns don't wear shorts. We don't wear flip flops and we certainly don't hug trees! Seriously, what's up with your flip flops? They would last as long chopping wood as a wink from me Aunt Sassy.

SAWDUNCE: And you'd scrape your wee toes!

CHOPWIT: A slip of the axe would cut them clean off.

SAWDUNCE: Ow.

PRESIDENT LEAFHOPPER: They're better than bare feet on hot cobblestone. And better than wearing clunky boots in my line of work! I like them. They slide right on. Comfortable. And they make funny noises. (*demonstrates*) But I'm not saying to wear my flip flops. I'm asking you to give democracy and me a chance.

AXESTORM: Ridiculous.

PRESIDENT LEAFHOPPER: How's your mayor?

AXESTORM: Huh? He's a dunce.

SAWDUNCE: That's not nice.

PRESIDENT LEAFHOPPER: And how was he chosen?

AXESTORM: He's the king's third cousin or something.

PRESIENT LEAFHOPPER. See, now that we have a democracy, you get to vote for the next one! You could elect a new mayor. That's why I'm asking for your support.

AXESTORM: You created tree cutting regulations and expect us to support you?

PRESIDENT LEAFHOPPER: For obvious reasons, limiting tree chopping is one the main reasons I won the election. But we can talk about that. I'd really like to win this contest. What do you propose?

AXESTORM: Unlimited tree chopping. No restrictions!

PRESIDENT LEAFHOPPER: I'm so glad we're having this conversation! Four trees per day isn't enough? But you already have so many trees just laying around. What are you doing with them? Seems like a waste, you've upset a lot of people, and you're running out of trees. But I'll talk to my people.

AXESTORM: And pay us double what the king did.

CHOPWIT: Yes!

PRESIDENT LEAFHOPPER: I'll tell you what. If you vote me as the winner of this contest, right now—where is the trophy by the way? —I'll make you a deal. I can confidently extend the chopping to eight trees per day. (*beat*) Per leprechaun.

AXESTORM: *Lumberjack* Leprechaun! Why don't you

make that change right now?

PRESIDENT LEAFHOPPER: Really need that win first.

AXESTORM: (*to BLARNEY*) Get this leafnut out of here!

PRESIDENT LEAFHOPPER: (*heading for the door with BODYGUARD*) Should I stick around? Prepare a victory speech as the presumptive next leader of the Lumberjack Leprechauns?

AXESTORM: Get out! (*they exit*)

CHOPWIT: Any discuss—

AXESTORM: Rate!

AXESTORM holds up a 1, CHOPWIT a 2, and SAWDUNCE a 5.

AXESTORM: You gave that four-leaf fraudster a 5?!

SAWDUNCE: After I scraped me wee hands, the open wounds remind me to keep an open mind. She had some good points. And she doubled the number of trees we can cut!

AXESTORM: We used to have unlimited tree chopping! And the king paid us!

CHOPWIT: That brings the total rating to 8. Not enough to make the leader board.

AXESTORM: Excellent. I know we'll have better luck with the next contestant!

Suddenly, SHEEP and his MOM are outside the door, arguing and competing for who will knock on the door.

SHEEP: Mom! Stop knocking for me—I can do it me self! I'm not wearing that costume. This is so stupid!

This teen SHEEP does not look anything like a sheep.
He is dressed in sloppy clothes covered with pieces of straw
and wearing huge green goggles strapped to his face—which
is a smart phone.
Note: MOM stays outside, perhaps never being seen or
occasionally poking her head into the door entrance. Mum
can be substituted for Mom if an Irish term is preferred.

AXESTORM: Blarney! Protocol!

BLARNEY: (*Steps outside*) Miss, please. Miss! (*pounds on the door*) Our next contestant is apparently dressed as a Sheep.

AXESTORM: You may enter, talent toter.

BLARNEY walks in wide-eyed, shaking his head.

SHEEP: (*shuffles in, itching his neck*). Stupid straw! *(He reaches out and swipes the air, apparently distracted by the interactive interior screen of the green goggles. He walks into table and lifts his goggles.)* Who put that there? (*He ignores judges, moves to the middle of the room, scratches his back, whines, and places goggles back on. He swipes the air and giggles.*) Good one. Stupid leafnuts.

CHOPWIT: You are a *sheep*?

SHEEP: (*ignores the question, swipes and pinches the air, and giggles*)

CHOPWIT: Are you a sheep? If so, that is the world's worst costume.

SHEEP: You're a sheep. (*scratches neck, arms, side*) I'm an independent thinker.

CHOPWIT: Are you here as a contestant for the next leader of the Lumberjack Leprechauns?

SHEEP: No. I mean, yeah, me mom made me. I'm

thirsty. (*lifts cell goggles to see*) Do you have anything to drink around here? (*scratches self, turns to door*) Because me mom forgot to pack drinks! (*slides goggles back into place*)

CHOPWIT: All out.

SHEEP: This party is lame.

CHOPWIT: This is not a party—it's a contest! What is your costume?

SHEEP: Bigfoot.

SAWDUNCE dives under the table.

MOM: Or he could be a wolf dressed in sheep's clothing! Get it? That's how you'll sneak into the castle!

SHEEP: Mom! I'm Bigfoot!

CHOPWIT: Ah. Thanks for clarifying. I thought you were a magical unicorn wearing green goggles.

AXESTORM: Yeah, smarty pants. Show some respect. Look at us when you talk.

SHEEP: You're a smarty pants. What do I get if I win the contest?

CHOPWIT: A pot o' gold bigger than this cabin.

AXESTORM: Chopwit!

SHEEP: Whoa. Really?

CHOPWIT: Oh, yeah. And that's just the beginning. You'll have power beyond your wildest dreams. You can order adults around like a video game. And they have to listen to you.

SHEEP: Whoa. If I had that much money and power, my friends and I would party every day!

SAWDUNCE: (*from underneath the table*) I love parties with lots of people!

SHEEP: You could totally crash my parties!

SAWDUNCE: Oh, thank you. I'll just walk into your party though. No stilt crashing for me. I scraped me wee hands—

CHOPWIT: Ahhh! But first Sheep, you must prove your leadership talent.

AXESTORM: You okay there, Chopwit?

CHOPWIT: Never been better. I'm just reminded of me bratty nieces and nephews who either ignore me or play tricks on me.

SHEEP: No, like seriously. What do I need to do to win? Wait, do I have to do work?

CHOPWIT: First, you need to shout that you love your mother.

SHEEP: Really? Mom, I love you.

CHOPWIT: Louder.

SHEEP: Mom, I love you!

CHOPWIT: She can't hear you.

SHEEP: Mom, I love you!!

MOM: What's wrong in there? Everything okay?

SHEEP: Yeah, I'm fine! Don't come in! I can do this me self!

CHOPWIT: Baaa like a sheep.

SHEEP: What?

CHOPWIT: Next contestant!

SHEEP: No! Baaa. Baaa.

CHOPWIT: (*to the other judges*) Is this contestant saying something?

SHEEP: Baaa! Baaa!

CHOPWIT: Louder!

SHEEP: Baaa!! Baaa!!

CHOPWIT: Very good. And now, for the greatest test of talent. (*beat*) You must stomp on your green goggles, crushing them into wee pieces.

SHEEP: What?! Why?

CHOPWIT: To build trust, we must know that you can sacrifice that which holds you back. And that which holds us back as Lumberjack Leprechauns.

SAWDUNCE: (*peeking head from underneath the table*) Those green goggles are holding us back!

SHEEP: That's not fair!

CHOPWIT: It is the only way. Wee pieces. Stomp them like Bigfoot.

SHEEP: That pot o' gold is as big as this cabin?

CHOPWIT: Maybe bigger.

SHEEP: Holy shamrocks. (*paces, places green goggles on the floor, contemplating a difficult decision*) I could buy a house that isn't made of straw! Imagine the parties! But my uncle—the guy who sold us our straw house—just bought these fancy green goggles for me. They stick to me face 24/7! Listen, seriously. We could dress like sheep wearing these goggles—because these sheep never stop wearing goggles—and we storm the castle!

CHOPWIT: Sorry, no goggles storming the castle. Unless you're making a documentary. Imagine, our leader charging with goggles! What could be more ridiculous?

SHEEP: No green goggles? This contest is stupid! (*snatches goggles off the floor*) Mom, I told you this was stupid! And forget what I said earlier! (*storms out*)

CHOPWIT: Any discussion?

AXESTORM: A bit rough on a leprechaun lad, don't you think?

CHOPWIT: I guess I have my triggers. And c'mon, he deserved it.

AXESTORM: Where do these contestants come

from?!

SAWDUNCE: (*returns to seat*) Is Bigfoot gone?

AXESTORM: Bigfoot isn't real!

AXESTORM holds up a 1, CHOPWIT a 1, and SAWDUNCE a 2.

CHOPWIT: That brings the total rating to 4.

SHEEP: (*outside*) Did I win?

MOM: Did he win?

SHEEP: Mom!

CHOPWIT: Oh, so sad. You're in dead last place! Sorry, you didn't quite make it to the leader board. Maybe you should be a sheep and listen to your mother. Better luck next time!

SHEEP: See I told you—I never win anything! Your party is as lame as a rainbow with no gold at the end!

CHOPWIT: Strangely, that is metaphorical for our contestant situation.

AXESTORM: This is not good. While our leader board contestants have unique strengths, I remain very doubtful that their costumes and abilities can successfully storm the castle and overthrow the leafnuts. How is it possible that we only have three qualified contestants for such a noble position and opportunity!

BLARNEY: Don't rule out the nurse—the best contestant by far! (*appeals to the audience*)

AXESTORM: But where are the true leaders of strength, cunning, and character? Leaders who wear castle-storming costumes. Leaders who can get the job done.

Suddenly, the judges and BLARNEY look up, hearing something crawling across the roof.

SAWDUNCE: What is that?!

AXESTORM: I don't know. But it sounds like a leader!

They track their heads with the imagined movements of the figure, which eventually leaps onto the ground beside the entrance door.

WILLOW *(pounds on the door. She is wearing tree climbing tactical gear that includes a grappling hook on the end of a rope.)*

AXESTORM: Blarney!

BLARNEY: *(Steps outside)* Oh, hello! *(knocks on the door)* Our next contestant is called Willow.

CHOPWIT: Clever!

AXESTORM: You may enter, talent toter.

WILLOW enters with swagger, twirling the grappling hook.

CHOPWIT: Aw. I thought you'd be dressed as a willow tree.

WILLOW: They are graceful, are they not?

CHOPWIT: See, that would have been hilarious because we're Lumberjack Leprechauns! And we could use some laughs! Especially Axestorm.

AXESTORM: *(grunts)*

WILLOW: *(grunts)*

CHOPWIT: We cut down trees. Get it?

WILLOW: I do. Believe me, I do.

CHOPWIT: You know, a better sense of humor could help get you elected as our next leader.

AXESTORM: What is your costume? What is that you're swinging?

WILLOW: I'm a very skilled climber. And this grappling hook that can wrap around a tree limb ever so carefully, so as not to scratch or damage even a twig. And with this trusty rope, I can climb to the top of any tree—willow, oak, pine, you name it—in ten seconds flat.

AXESTORM: While I would appreciate your hyperbole in a different context, such as a pub on St. Patrick's Day, this is a serious contest.

WILLOW: I am as serious as a tree that flattens a lumberjack.

SAWDUNCE: Ouch.

CHOPWIT: Prove it.

WILLOW: Let's go outside.

They all go outside. WILLOW quickly climbs a tall tree.

CHOPWIT: No way!

AXESTORM: I don't believe it!

SAWDUNCE: Hooray!

The Judges all return enthusiastically. WILLOW enters with vindicated swagger.

AXESTORM: That was, that was incredible! You shot up that tall tree faster than a fairy on fairy dust.

CHOPWIT: 8.3 seconds to the top. Unbelievable.

SAWDUNCE: (*tugging at bandages*) We could really use someone like you.

AXESTORM: Yes. Could you teach others to do that?

Or perhaps an entire region of Lumberjack Leprechauns?

WILLOW: Of course. Under the right conditions. And with the right understanding.

CHOPWIT: Where are you going with this Axestorm? I can see your wee wheels turning.

AXESTORM: That tree was taller than the castle wall. Could you train us to climb the castle wall?

CHOPWIT: Genius!

WILLOW: Easily. I've done it several times, just for fun. And indeed—I can see the genius in this room. You understood my plan to storm the castle before I revealed it.

AXESTORM: Don't excite me without reason! Are you joking?

WILLOW: I'm not the joking type.

AXESTORM: Thank you. You scaled the castle wall, just for fun? And you reached the other side?!

WILLOW: Yes. If you include the descent, it took about 30 seconds. The castle walls are more difficult to climb than trees, unless the tree is a hawthorn.

SAWDUNCE: And you didn't scrape your hands?

WILLOW: On tree thorns?

SAWDUNCE: On the castle walls.

WILLOW: Why would I do that? (*glancing at SAWDUNCE's bandages*) I can see that this training will not be easy. Perhaps I should leave.

AXESTORM: No! Don't you want to win this contest? And lead our mission?

WILLOW: Where I lead, you are not prepared to follow.

CHOPWIT: We can learn! Just give us a chance.

WILLOW: You are too weak. Too scared. Too certain.

SAWDUNCE: No, we're not! We're ready to change! We're ready to question anything!

WILLOW: I understand that you want to storm the castle from your contest flyer, but I don't understand why. What is your mission exactly?

AXESTORM: I can see that you are a trustworthy ally. And so, I will tell you. We intend to overthrow the leafnuts, restore the monarchy, and return to unlimited tree chopping.

WILLOW: And why would you want to do that? There are so many dead trees strewn across regions of the Lumberjack Leprechauns. Why not use the trees that have already given their lives? At some point, there will be no trees left.

AXESTORM: If you must know, eventually we will prove victorious and find the long-lost great pot o' gold, buried many generations ago, now covered and tangled with tree roots.

WILLOW: It's not at the end of a rainbow?

SAWDUNCE: Ha! Willow does have a sense of humor!

AXESTORM: What? No, this is the mother of all pots o' gold, hidden under trees. It's bigger than this cabin! That's why the king paid us to find it!

WILLOW: And that's why you've been cutting down trees all these years? For generations.

SAWDUNCE: How do you know about cutting down trees for generations? Willow is a psychic!

WILLOW: Hardly. Just a keen observer. I should go.

AXESTORM: No! No. Not now. I've told you everything! If this information got into the wrong hands… Back to the training. We are willing to do whatever it takes!

WILLOW: Anything?

The judges nod yes seriously.

WILLOW: Then we will start now. Cry like a hawk that's lost its nest.
SAWDUNCE: I don't like hawks.
WILLOW: Cry like a hawk!
AXESTORM: It's a test!

The judges cry like hawks.

WILLOW: Hop like a squirrel that's lost its home!

The judges hop like squirrels.

WILLOW: I don't believe you! These squirrels are very sad!

The judges hop like depressed squirrels.

CHOPWIT: Why am I feeling a strange sense of deja vu?
WILLOW: Oh, you've never been where I'm going to take you! Now say, "I can't wait to find me pot o' gold!" and run into the door.

The judges exchange confused glances.

WILLOW: Do it!

The judges follow orders, falling down when they hit the door, wincing and cursing.

SAWDUNCE: Why did you make us do that?!

WILLOW: As you have wisely surmised, this is a small test of your bravery. But there is one final test, before I leave you to consider me as your next leader. Grab your axes.

AXESTORM: Finally, a test that makes sense!

The judges grab their axes and return.

WILLOW: Chop off each other's fingers.

The judges scream.

SAWDUNCE: Why?!

WILLOW: It is the only way.

The judges scream.

CHOPWIT: Why does this feel familiar?

WILLOW: It is the only way!!

The judges scream.

WILLOW: Unless.

The judges breathe a sigh of relief.

CHOPWIT: Unless?

WILLOW: No. You are too weak.

AXESTORM: We are not weak! We are strong Lumberjack Leprechauns!

WILLOW: You must face your greatest fear.

SAWDUNCE: Bigfoot is real?!

WILLOW: Fool! You must cease chopping trees for one year.

AXESTORM: Sacrilegious, Bigfoot, gold stealing, bad luck monster! Your training is too extreme!

WILLOW: And instead, plant ten trees for every tree that you cut down.

AXESTROM. It makes no sense! That's the complete opposite of—

WILLOW: It makes perfect sense! Listen closely. The sapling that first reaches 30 meters will tell you where the gold is hidden.

AXESTORM: What? I don't understand.

WILLOW: (*trying not to laugh*) Listen closely. Because those roots will be closest to the gold. You've been using the wrong method all these years. The older trees don't reveal the gold's location because they've already grown. But the fastest growing new trees will expose the hidden spot!

SAWDUNCE: Is that true?

CHOPWIT: How could we not know this? Why is this funny?

AXESTORM: (*beat*) Tree Hugger!!!

WILLOW: So close! (*runs outside*)

CHOPWIT: (*tries to chase, held back by AXESTORM*) I can't believe that we just fell for—

AXESTORM: Let the Tree Hugger go! It's another trick for us to follow, probably with a fool's gold trap! We must stay focused on finding The Golden One.

CHOPWIT: Protocol! Further discussion?

AXESTORM: Rate!

AXESTORM holds up a 1, CHOPWIT a 1, and SAWDUNCE a 3.

AXESTORM: A three?! That Tree Hugger told you to cut off your wee fingers!

SAWDUNCE: I'm a strengths-based rater. Strong tree climbing skills.

AXESTORM: It was a *Tree Hugger*! The enemy of all enemies! Worse than the leafnuts! And of course it can climb trees!

CHOPWIT: Regardless, at five points, Willow did not make the leader board. Maybe we should call it a day and cut our losses.

SAWDUNCE: Strangely, I'm feeling lucky about our next contestant.

AXESTORM: Yes, let's trust the intuition of a Lumberjack Leprechaun who just gave a Tree Hugger three points. (*beat*) Oh, please great Mother of Gold and double rainbows, deliver us a truly worthy contestant.

Dramatic change in atmosphere. A powerful wind blows. The Judges and BLARNEY rush to look out the window.

AXESTORM: Might be a storm coming.

SAWDUNCE: Maybe we'll see a rainbow.

Wind calms. Bright sunlight shines. A GUIDE walks unnoticed through the door, wearing a robe.

CHOPWIT: There's the sun, peeking through the clouds!

The Judges and BLARNEY turn around to find the GUIDE standing serene and grounded.

41

BLARNEY: Whoa. That's not the protocol, buddy!

AXESTORM: Exit the door, and return with the talent—

GUIDE: You are all going to die.

SAWDUNCE dives under the table. AXESTORM raises an axe, ready to fight.

CHOPWIT: (*stands up, clutching an axe*) An assassination attempt! The Tree Huggers are on to us!

GUIDE: (*chuckling*) One day. One day you are all going to die.

SAWDUNCE: (*from behind the table*) Not today?

GUIDE: Not today. But reflecting on mortality can bring life great meaning.

AXESTORM: Are you with a new sect of the leafnuts?

GUIDE: No.

CHOPWIT: Who are you? Another Tree Hugger? Oh, the lengths they will go to disguise themselves!

GUIDE: Who are you? An important question to contemplate within our time space reality.

AXESTORM: We are having a serious costume contest to select the next leader of the Lumberjack Leprechauns! There's no time to answer silly questions! What is your costume?

GUIDE: My small, separate self?

CHOPWIT: Watch it!

SAWDUNCE: Is he making fun of our size?

AXESTORM: Are you here to lead us?

GUIDE: I am a guide to help you lead yourselves.

SAWDUNCE: Are you a guide sent from the Mother

of Gold? Should we bow?

GUIDE: Please don't.

AXESTORM: Sawdunce has sniffed you out! A fake contestant. Blarney, throw out this fool!

GUIDE: I will leave after everyone has asked their big question.

BLARNEY: Let's go fruitcake. (*attempts to move the GUIDE to the door, who doesn't budge*) This Guide is as solid as a tree.

Upbeat Irish music something like the Swallowtail Jig plays. AXESTORM and CHOPWIT jump in, trying to move, push, pull, or tackle the GUIDE, but each attempt is met with a smooth, graceful block, arm twist, turn, or throw, where attacks are redirected into dance turns and spins. SAWDUNCE cheerily dances and claps by himself. Finally, AXESTORM and CHOPWIT give up and return to their seats. Music fades.

AXESTORM: Let us hear from this strange yet strong contestant. You want to be the next leader of the Lumberjack Leprechauns?

GUIDE: That is not your big question.

AXESTORM: Right, robed guru. Who put you up to this—the Tree Huggers, the leafnuts? The owl?

SAWDUNCE: The wise owl, I think!

AXESTORM: (*stands up, paces*) Are you with the leafnuts? Or the Tree Huggers?!

GUIDE: I cannot separate myself from the Leaf People, Tree Huggers, Lumberjack Leprechauns, woodland creatures, or trees any more than a wave can separate itself from the ocean. We dwell within the same planet, the same galaxy, and the same universe. But that is not your big question.

AXESTORM: How am I possibly the same as a leafnut? Those idiots must be overthrown!

GUIDE: I didn't say you were the same. But you do share the same fundamental essence. And once you realize this, the Leaf People and Tree Huggers won't be such a bother. But that is not your big question.

AXESTORM: Okay nutty Guide. And how would I notice this supposed essence?

GUIDE: Who is the talker talking, right now? Who is the walker walking, right now? Who is the observer observing, right now?

CHOPWIT: (*excited*) Are you referring to collective consciousness?

AXESTORM and SAWDUNCE exchange confused, worried glances.

CHOPWIT: What? I read books. Can't a leprechaun read?

GUIDE: It is known by many names across many wisdom traditions.

CHOPWIT: I thought that was the stuff of fairy folklore! If only I had more than five books to read.

AXESTORM: Is this new age malarkey?

GUIDE: Ha! This wisdom has existed for eons. And yet, the great teachers of the past are not asking us to return to some mythical fantasy land; rather, they are still pointing to the future. But don't take my word for it. Learn and recognize it for yourself. You are already connected to everything within a seamless universe. You are walking through a doorless door, you just don't notice it. But that is not your big question. Find the courage to ask it.

AXESTORM: Okay, you want to know my big question? Where is the pot o' gold that my great, great, great grandfather buried?

GUIDE: That is not your big question.

AXESTORM: Ahhh! I wonder why I'm so angry?!

SAWDUNCE: Axestorm is often angry.

GUIDE: Suffering is a cry from a soul ready to change. But that is not your big question.

AXESTORM: Where is the pot o' gold is my big question! It's the question I've been asking since I was a wee lad! It's the question that my father, and his father, and his father have been asking for generations!

GUIDE: Why do you want to find the gold?

AXESTORM: What? To support the king. And to be rich of course!

GUIDE: Why do you want to be rich?

AXESTORM: Stop asking these ridiculous questions! Are the answers not self-evident? (*starting to break down*) Ahh, can we be done with this? Here you go: I want to be rich to completely change me life! I'll have time to learn decent carpentry skills without hammering me wee thumb, to finally build a decent home for me wee kids that isn't made of scratchy straw that blows all over tarnation, to care for me sick wife, to pay Chopwit properly for his delicious brew, and to play cards with my friends any time I want. That's why I need the gold. Where is the gold?!

GUIDE: That is not your big question. The gold you seek lies within.

AXESTORM: Let me tell you where I'll stuff that golden idea. Ahh! How do we defeat the leafnuts and Tree Huggers?!

GUIDE: Ahh indeed. You were heading in the right direction, and then made a U-turn and retreated back to your old thinking. Have you considered that perhaps you are trying to solve the wrong problem?

AXESTORM: This is torture!

GUIDE: Yes, painful learning now can create profound joy later. But how to defeat the Leaf People is not your big question.

AXESTORM: Ahhh!

GUIDE: Are these not your true friends who sit beside you? Friends you trust with your life each day. You have nothing to fear. Chop down your resistance! Listen to your inner voice.

AXESTORM: (*turns to CHOPWIT and SAWDUNCE, who encourage him*) Didn't see this one coming.

GUIDE: What does your deepest self really want to ask?

AXESTORM: I want to... I want to know; how can I be happy?! How can I enjoy me life and family? How can I earn a living building things?

CHOPWIT: I thought you liked being a lumberjack? I had no idea you wanted to build things.

AXESTORM: Ah, you know, ever since that time I hammered me thumb as a wee lad trying to build a bird house, and me father laughed at me and reminded me of the king's orders to find the buried great pot o' gold, I turned to chopping wood instead of building with it. Timber. Ha, ha.

GUIDE: (*nods, then turns to CHOPWIT*) And what is your big question?

CHOPWIT: I'm here because of me friends. I'm a lumberjack because of me friends. But, I mean, if we found that pot o' gold, I'd love to buy me own pub and sell me lucky golden brew. But this wouldn't be any pub, it would have room for dancing, stand-up comedy, and it would have a bookstore. A pub that feeds the body, the heart, and the mind, if you know what I mean.

AXESTORM: I like that idea.

SAWDUNCE: I'd love that place! Maybe you could teach me to read?

CHOPWIT: Of course. (*to AXESTORM*) And maybe you could help me build me pub? And not a straw one.

AXESTORM: Well, I think we have enough timber. (*turns to SAWDUNCE*) And what about you? What is your big question?

SAWDUNCE: Nah, mine's stupid.

CHOPWIT: Oh, come on. We're bearing our souls here Sawdunce! Open up already!

SAWDUNCE: Well, I have two. My first question is, How do I change me name? I'm sharper than what people think. For example, I notice that the leprechauns go to work passing each other, and the kids go to school, or work, with their green goggles, but we aren't talking to each other. And then we all come home, passing each other like lost, floating boats drifting without a purpose. I'm not sure any of us are very happy. Maybe it's because there's no place to gather. So, I was just thinking, that if Chopwit started a pub, then maybe... Ah, never mind. You'll need help tending the bar or stacking books, right? Maybe you can give me a job.

CHOPWIT: Go on! What is your big, bold question?

SAWDUNCE: Well, after I scraped me wee hands, I

was thinking, like I do in me brain, even if no one knows, How could we as a leprechaun community build a space together? An incredible space for gathering. A space for games, a space for reading, dancing, and laughing! Maybe a proper football field. Maybe we'd talk to each other. Maybe you would even have some fun, Axestorm. Maybe this place would have a pony farm. Me kids love riding ponies, the miniature-sized ones.

AXESTORM: That's a fantastic idea! We need that.

SAWDUNCE: Yeah, and you know what leprechauns are going to want in this space? (*turns to CHOPWIT*) A pub with mind-blowing brew, food, and books.

CHOPWIT: Maybe you should run for office now that we have a democracy, Mayor.

AXESTORM: Yeah, I think so! You've got two votes already!

SAWDUNCE: Ha. Well, then. You can call me Mayor Sawblade.

BLARNEY (*walks over*) Eh hem.

SAWDUNCE: Blarney! Forgot you were here. What's your big question?

BLARNEY: That's simple. How do I find the love of me life? And how do I travel the world? But first, I'll vote for you, too, Mayor Sawblade.

AXESTORM: Is this happening?! Are we seriously thinking about changing our entire lives because of this Guide dressed in a robe?

GUIDE: I've done little. You discovered who was already there.

CHOPWIT: What about the contest? What about storming the castle? We have a protocol. (*Judges rush to the table*) Wait, what are we even rating? For the Guide to be our leader?

GUIDE: You know what you're doing.

SAWDUNCE: We're determining whether to lead our own lives, whether to change our mission!

CHOPWIT: Aww. I was looking forward to storming the castle without stilts.

AXESTORM: What about the leafnuts?! We can't be ruled by the leafnuts! I can't stand those flip flops.

CHOPWIT: You don't have to wear flip flops! Maybe we should give this democracy a chance.

AXESTORM: What about the great pot o' gold? How are we going to pay for our dreams to come true? You can't build that pub with fairy dust.

SAWDUNCE: Of course we want a pot o' gold! But what if we're thrown in the dungeon with Stumpsharp for storming the castle? And even if we were successful, why do we think we can find the great pot o' gold that no one has found in over 100 years! Maybe it doesn't even exist.

AXESTORM: Careful now.

SAWDUNCE: My point is, I don't want to waste another moment. Let's rate already!

CHOPWIT: We can do this Axestorm. It's time to vote for leading our own lives, for starting an adventure that leads to our real dreams.

BLARNEY: (*encourages audience to boo*) An interesting contestant, but still no match for the Nurse!

SAWDUNCE triumphantly holds up a 10, CHOPWIT a 9, and AXESTORM a 7.

CHOPWIT: 26 total points! (*records on leader board*) By far the leading choice. Are we ready to bring out the finalists?

GUIDE: (*peering outside*) No. You will first face a great test. (*suddenly grabs SAWDUNCE and AXESTORM, smashing all three judges together and pulling them in closely*) Choosing your new leader is a big deal, which could ignite a supernova of good fortune, or create a black hole of despair. Choose wisely. (*GUIDE exits, thunder rumbles in this distance*)

AXESTORM: Where'd the Guide go? Stick around! (*no response*) Wait. Procedural question—does the Guide need to be present for the final decision?

CHOPWIT: Technically, no, because we wouldn't be choosing the Guide to lead us, we'd be choosing to lead ourselves. We're The Golden Ones!

AXESTORM: I suddenly feel… scared. Leading our own lives? That's a lot of responsibility! Sometimes I just want the king to tell me what to do.

SAWDUNCE: We can do this! But what did the Guide mean, we will face a great test?

AXESTORM: Not another Tree Hugger!

BLARNEY: I think we should bring out the finalists!

SAWDUNCE: Yes, why wait?

CHOPWIT: Let's select our next leader!

AXESTORM: Why can we not have a clear choice?

SAWDUNCE: We have all the information we need! Let's do this!

Dramatic change in atmosphere. A powerful wind blows. Skies darken. Thunder rumbles closer.

AXESTORM: Thunder! A sign from the universe!

THUMPER: (*knocks on the door with head butts*)

THUMPER has traveled a great distance from Puddin'

Head Island and is lost. He is on a mission to defeat the Sweeties, who wear the color blue, and are the enemy of true red Puddin' Heads. He is wearing a bright red shirt, sea monster boots, a spoon helmet (or pan, with the handle facing backward), spoon armor, a backpack, and a spoon belt with each side holding four spoons: small, medium, large, and very large.

SAWDUNCE: The great test!

AXESTORM: This could be The Golden One! (*waves wildly at BLARNEY*) Go!

BLARNEY: (*exits, then pounds on the door*) Our next character—and he is a character! —I mean, our next contestant, is called Thumper. And I have no idea what costume he is wearing.

AXESTORM: You may enter, talent toter.

THUMPER struts confidently into and around the room, studies and owns the room, his spoons jangling with each proud stride.

THUMPER: Plenty of red. Green is tolerable. And no sign of blue. This is very promising. (*approaches Sawdunce. Picks up a thin stick leaning against the wall, studying it.*) Nice.

SAWDUNCE: It's a walking stick I picked up in the woods for me kid.

THUMPER: May I? (*head butts the thin stick in half with bravado, tossing it to the side*)

SAWDUNCE: Hey—

AXESTORM: Amazing. Who are you?

THUMPER: I am Thumper, the all-time, greatest true red Puddin' Head leader from Puddin' Head Island, Region 5, Island Nation. I was returning from a conspiracy conference—of course, I was the keynote speaker—and must have, uh, taken a wrong left turn heading to the airport. Where am I?

CHOPWIT: You were at a conference, took a wrong turn, and wound up *here*?

THUMPER: Yes. I believe that everything happens for a reason.

AXESTORM: Agree. Love your costume, but what in tarnation are you wearing? What's up with the spoons? Why is a pan strapped to your head?

THUMPER: Costume? You don't have spoon weapons here? This combat gear is essential for defeating the enemy. (*pulling spoons from spoon belt*) The small spoon is to deflect enemy fire; the medium spoon—

CHOPWIT: What kind of spoons?

THUMPER: The most powerful spoons in the world! (*thunderclaps are closer*)

AXESTORM: It is a sign!

THUMPER: As I was saying, the medium spoon is to eat puddin'; the large spoon is an all-purpose weapon; and the extra-large spoon is to cover your eyes if surrounded by the enemy. They go for the eyes first. But not if you charge with large spoons, correctly. (lifts both large spoons above his head and demonstrates charging around the room) Ahhhhh!

SAWDUNCE: What about lightening?

THUMPER: (*stops*) It does strike spoons occasionally. It can be very unpleasant, especially if frying the spoon helmet, which of course, is the most important weapon of all. Under typical weather conditions, it provides superior protection and head butting. (*beat*) It is no *pan*.

CHOPWIT: Strange. Do Puddin' Heads run out of spoons?

THUMPER: Never! What do you think this backpack is for? (*slips off backpack and pulls out a handful of spoons*) Backup spoons!

CHOPWIT: Right. Tell us about your boots.

THUMPER: (*peeks under the judge's table*) You aren't wearing sea monster boots? These are the greatest boots in the world! Not comfortable, but oh do they terrify the enemy!

AXESTORM: Excellent. And so much better than flip flops!

NURSE: (*outside*) Water. Water!

THUMPER: Say, might you have something to drink? There is a pathetic nurse outside.

CHOPWIT: We're all out, but there is a water pump outside.

BLARNEY: We have a water pump?! (*runs outside*)

CHOPWIT: What about you? You must be parched from that arduous journey.

THUMPER: I won't eat or drink until I've built a coalition that can crush the Sweeties.

AXESTORM: A leader of nobility, sacrifice, and strength. Who are the Sweeties?

THUMPER: Oh, it pains me to even say that word. They are the evil enemy of Puddin' Heads. They spread kindness, wear the color blue, lay around all day eating cookies and cake, and their offspring are all wusses.

SAWDUNCE: I love cookies.

THUMPER: No! Cookies are for Sweeties, who also, by the way, set spoon traps that are nearly impossible to escape! Unless you are trained by the greatest trainer in the world—me!

AXESTORM: The Sweeties sound like the cousins of the leafnuts! Or Tree Huggers.

THUMPER: Great Mother of Puddin'! You have Tree Huggers here, too? They are the worst of all Sweeties, leaping to and fro, and surprisingly fierce fighters.

CHOPWIT: I thought Sweeties were all wusses.

THUMPER: This Sweetie sect mutated into zombies disguised as Tree Huggers. It is the only logical explanation.

SAWDUNCE: (*scared*) Zombies?

THUMPER: Yes. Of course, the Sweetie conspiracy to take over the world is true, but I never expected them to populate and spread so quickly! I must tell my island immediately. I must stop the new ludicrous idea that is spreading like an indoctrinating plague.

AXESTORM: What is this outrageous idea?

THUMPER: That Puddin' Heads and Sweeties should get along! It must be crushed along with the tree-hugging zombies. How serendipitous that I discovered you.

AXESTORM: Serendipity indeed.

THUMPER: Everything happens for a reason.

AXESTORM: (*excited*) How will you storm the castle?

THUMPER: Storm the castle?

AXESTORM: Storm the castle, overthrow the leafnuts—ahh, and the Tree Huggers even though they aren't really in charge—appoint you as The Golden One, abolish deforesting regulations, and cut down trees until we find the long-lost great pot o' gold!

THUMPER: The Golden One? I like the ring of that. (*whacks spoon on helmet*) Tell me about this castle.

AXESTORM: It is impenetrable. It is surrounded by a deep moat with sea monsters—

SAWDUNCE: The moat has sea monsters?! No one told me that!

AXESTORM: They nap in the afternoon. Thus, our strategic daytime attack. Anyway, there is a deep moat with sea monsters, and very, very tall walls. Our stilts were of no use.

SAWDUNCE: I scraped me wee hands!

AXESTORM: It has a draw bridge that rarely opens and a metal entrance door that is as thick as a tree. Our axes were of no use, either.

CHOPWIT: We lost many axes.

THUMPER: (*glancing at the door*) Thick as one tree, eh? That won't be a problem. Two trees, maybe. But one is child's play. (*walks over to the door, swiftly head butts it, and the door swings open, or better, falls over*)

AXESTORM: Great Mother of Gold! How did you do that? It must be the spoon helmet!

THUMPER: That is a common misconception. While the spoon helmet is essential in delivering a powerful blow, it's really about proper technique. It happened so fast, you probably missed it. If you had watched closely, you would see how I shot out my arms holding spoons, rocked back slightly, and then unleashed my torso for a solid strike. (*demonstrates*) People think it's about spoon helmets, or thick heads, or neck speed—all of which help, of course. But fundamentally, head butting power is generated from your core.

SAWDUNCE: (*examines the door*) It's a sign! The Guide's premonition—walk through the doorless door!

BLARNEY: (*returns, walks through the open door*) What'd

I miss?

CHOPWIT: Talent beyond your comprehension. (*to Thumper*) But the castle door is easily ten times as thick and tall. You can't possibly knock that door down by yourself.

THUMPER: You are wise. I know my limitations. And I also know that with 20, eh, maybe 50 trained Leprechauns stacked on top of each other—

AXESTORM: Especially Lumberjack Leprechauns.

THUMPER: Yes, especially with Lumberjack Leprechauns, wearing spoon helmets, wielding the strongest spoons in the world—

AXESTORM: Go on!

THUMPER: And with specialized training from myself—the greatest leader in the world—all head butting the castle door at the same precise moment… that door will fall like a tall tree.

AXESTORM: (*falls to knees, bowing*) Great leader!

SAWDUNCE: I thought the king was the great leader.

AXESTORM: They are both great leaders!

SAWDUNCE: But the king isn't a leader anymore.

AXESTORM: Ahhh! But he will be after our new great leader storms the castle!

THUMPER: I warn you: Do not accept me as your great leader unless you are ready to join a bold mission, a mission that is not for the faint of heart! Speaking of which, we should charge at night.

SAWDUNCE: Scary!

CHOPWIT: Ridiculous. How would we see?

SAWDUNCE: Wait—green goggle night vision! We could recruit an army of SHEEP:

CHOPWIT: I like it! But let's not get ahead of ourselves. We have a protocol for selecting the next leader of the Lumberjack Leprechauns around here.

SAWDUNCE: Yeah, what about leading ourselves?

BLARNEY: And what about the Nurse?

AXESTORM: Those are secondary leaders. Think about it! We need that great pot o' gold to make our dreams come true! And now we're so close— we've finally found The Golden One, who will lead us in storming the castle, charging with spoon helmets and spoon weapons. Imagine the look on the leafnuts' faces. Imagine the swift victory. I'm sure Thumper could persuade the king to appoint you as mayor. Why have an election if you can just take power?

THUMPER: Indeed.

SAWDUNCE: Maybe. But this is the last time!

CHOPWIT: Protocol!

AXESTORM: Ah, all this hope has clouded my thinking—how could I forget? Further discussion! (*to THUMPER*) Your leadership skills are commendable. But how will we cross the moat?

SAWDUNCE: Good question! No more stilts!

THUMPER: You do not have spoon catapults?

AXESTORM: Spoon catapults?

THUMPER: (*Unholsters spoon. Searches the trash and pulls out wadded up cup, places it in the spoon bowl, and flings it over AXESTORM's head*) Understand?

AXESTORM: I am trying. Perhaps this strategy would work with a strong tailwind blowing at the castle. However, while I know that the leafnuts are idiotic twigs, I don't see how bombarding them with cups will make them open the draw bridge.

THUMPER: We won't ask for permission. My talented colleagues in Puddin' Head Region 4 have developed enormous spoon catapults to combat sea monsters off the coast of Puddin' Head Horn. Although we've never seen a sea monster, we are exceptionally well trained for the inevitable invasion attempt. These catapults are secured on movable platforms for swift transport and battle positioning. They are precise weapons of war that can easily launch humans, leprechauns, logs, buckets of smashed cups, hard rocks, sea monster boots, you name it, to any location into the moat, over the moat, or even over castle walls.

AXESTORM: Ah! Catapults can launch *large* objects! The Guide was right—we were solving the wrong problem! The problem is not how to build taller stilts, the problem is how to clear the castle wall! We've been thinking too small.

SAWDUNCE: But Willow solved that problem with a grappling hook and rope.

AXESTORM: Tree Huggers aren't going to solve our problems!

THUMPER: I should probably mention that catapult training has only been successful with humans landing in water; we haven't yet landed on land without broken bones. But then again, we haven't launched leprechauns, which definitely would work.

CHOPWIT: Why would leprechauns be successful?

THUMPER: (*grabs CHOPWIT's hat, demonstrates*) You have hats for parachutes!

AXESTORM: (*falls to knees*) The Golden One!

CHOPWIT: Protocol! Any further discussion?

SAWDUNCE: This is just to see if Thumper makes the leader board, right?

CHOPWIT: Correct. Then we must reach consensus on the next leader of the Lumberjack

Leprechauns!

AXESTORM: (*to THUMPER*) Wait outside. We won't be long!

THUMPER exits. AXESTORM holds up a 10, CHOPWIT a 9, and SAWDUNCE a 7.

AXESTORM: Only a 7?!

SAWDUNCE: Yeah. Thumper was an original. But I'm still leaning toward leading ourselves.

AXESTORM: You idiot! How can we lead ourselves or make our dreams come true without the gold? Have you thought this through?

SAWDUNCE: Finding the great pot o' gold would be nice.

CHOPWIT: 26 total points! (*records on leader board*) A tie for first place. It's time to bring out the finalists! It all comes down to this. The moment we've all been waiting for. Five finalists: Pig, Nurse, Owl, Ourselves, and Thumper. We will bring each contestant out in this order, hear closing arguments, and reach consensus on the next leader of the Lumberjack Leprechauns!

AXESTORM: (*to BLARNEY*) Get the Pig!

BLARNEY: Got it. (*exits through the door. Moments later, he returns with PIG and begins to walk through the entrance*)

Note: If the door is lying on the floor from THUMPER's previous head butt, BLARNEY begins to walk through the previous location of the door, which is now doorless.

AXESTORM: Protocol!

BLARNEY: (*sighs, exits, and knocks*) I have the first

finalist, who is dressed and smells like a Pig.

AXESTORM: You may enter, talent toter.

PIG: If you were leaning toward the Nurse, she just passed out.

BLARNEY: No! (*runs outside*)

CHOPWIT: Any discussion?

PIG: So, here's a deal you can't refuse. Elect me as your next leader and not only will I give you that great pot o' gold after my ponies plow it up, I will build you each a free straw mansion.

SAWDUNCE: Straw is itchy.

AXESTORM: Oh, I hate me straw house. The wind is always blowing it down. And there I go—gathering the roof, and the shingles, and patching them back together. If only it had a wooden frame.

PIG: This straw mansion would be ten times the size of your silly house.

AXESTORM: Ah, I don't care about a straw mansion —I care about the great pot o' gold! How can we trust that you'll actually find it when we've been searching for generations?

PIG: Oh, didn't I tell you? Not only can my very special ponies storm castles and plow for buried gold, they've been trained to sniff for gold, like pigs sniff for truffles.

SAWDUNCE: I love truffles!

CHOPWIT: Tempting, but how will your ponies storm the castle without magical flying powers?

PIG: Uhhh. If there's anyone in this room who isn't a leafnut, or a Tree Hugger, it is me, Jack Ham!

AXESTORM: Ahh! This is going to be a tough decision. Can the universe not give us a sign if Pig should be our new leader?

BLARNEY: (*swiftly returns, attempts to have the audience*

boo)

The judges take in the audience response, as if the popularity of this candidate may influence their decision.

BLARNEY: (*exits with PIG, knocks on the door*) I have the most talented finalist, dressed as a Nurse:

AXESTORM: You may enter, talent toter.

NURSE: (*enters with BLARNEY, parched*) So hot! Your pump water is nasty—somehow, it made me more thirsty! (*to Blarney*) I can't do this much longer.

BLARNEY: But you could be The Golden One.

NURSE: I don't think you understand how thirsty I am.

BLARNEY: Thirsty for someone special to join you…
In a meadow green, 'neath a rainbow's sheen,
Lived a leprechaun, small and quite unseen.
With a heart so bold, for a nurse he pined,
In those eyes so kind, his pot of gold he'd find.
Together they'd live, in a land of their own,
With a love so true, it's never been known.
Our lives will thrive, under skies so blue,
For my heart, dear nurse—

NURSE: (*pulls BLARNEY close*) Who just wants a mug of brew.

CHOPWIT: (*to judges*) Okay! Still not a limerick. Any further discussion?

AXESTORM: This nurse will be lucky to reach the castle, let alone storm the castle.

BLARNEY: This is the best leader we've seen yet. Look at the endurance! A remarkable performance, don't you think? (*appeals to the audience to cheer*)

The judges take in the audience response, as if the
popularity of this candidate may influence their decision.

AXESTORM: Next!

BLARNEY: (*exits hopeful with NURSE, then knocks on*
door) The next lousy finalist is dressed as an Owl.

AXESTORM: You may enter, talent toter.

OWL: (*flies into the room*)

Listen up, leprechauns of the wood,

An owl leader would be very good,

I'll keep our trees safe and sound,

With my keen eyesight, threats are found,

Trust in me, our forest's future looks good.

CHOPWIT: Not your best limerick. Any discussion?

AXESTORM: Does anyone here really think we
should select someone dressed as Owl as the next
leader of the Lumberjack Leprechauns?

BLARNEY attempts to have the audience boo. The
judges take in the audience response, as if the popularity
of this candidate may influence their decision.

AXESTORM: Next!

BLARNEY: (*exits with OWL, knocks on door*) The next
contestant is… You.

AXESTORM: You may enter, talent toter.

BLARNEY: (*enters, shrugs*)

CHOPWIT: Any discussion?

SAWDUNCE: Yes. I had an epiphany with the Guide.
For the first time, I actually believed my dream to
build a real community, for you, for me, for all of
us. And you, Chopwit, could have your own
delicious brew pub with a bookstore and a place to
dance and laugh. And you, Axestorm, could

become a skillful carpenter and builder. And you Blarney, well, I guess you're leaving us. But the rest of us, we could work together with real purpose to benefit all leprechauns!

CHOPWIT: Yes, and you could be our next mayor.

AXESTORM: Yes, yes, yes. That all sounds very fine. Oh, great universe, what a difficult decision!

SAWDUNCE: Let it go, Axestorm. Let's move on with our lives. Let's build the future we've been dreaming of.

AXESTORM: I'll consider it. But do we have what it takes to lead? (*turning to audience*) Should we choose ourselves as the new leaders of the Lumberjack Leprechauns?

BLARNEY: (*starts to influence the audience to boo, then stops abruptly, turning to the judges*) You're not going to choose the Nurse, are you?

AXESTORM: No decision has been predetermined. You know that.

BLARNEY: What am I doing? (*addressing judges and audience*) It's been a journey friends. And now, I'm going on one of me own. The next time we're together, it better be celebrating Mayor Sawblade's victory, in Chopwit's pub, that was built by Axestorm. Best of luck. Choose The Golden One wisely. (*exits*)

AXESTORM: Blarney!

SAWDUNCE: (*rushes after Blarney, returns*) I don't know what happened to the Pig, but Blarney just ran off with the Nurse, who's carrying a jug of lucky golden brew.

CHOPWIT: That's a disqualification. Finalists must be present to win.

AXESTORM: Who is going to chop wood and carry

water for us in the woods? What about the talent
toter protocol? Who will escort our most promising
finalist—

THUMPER: (*enters with confidence. Thunderclaps are closer.
Battle music plays softly, then grows louder*) Comrades.

CHOPWIT: Where is that music coming from?

AXESTORM: Is it a sign? Thumper, your battlefield
tactics, ingenious plan, and undeniable leadership
talent have clearly made you the front runner for
the leader of the Lumberjack Leprechauns. Alas,
we have other strong contestants, including
ourselves. Remind us why we should choose you.

CHOPWIT: Yes, why should we choose you over a,
uh, Pig or an Owl? Oh, let's be real. Why should
we choose you over Ourselves? We have finally
recognized our dreams, and believe it or not,
perhaps we do not need you as a leader.

SAWDUNCE: Yeah, why should we choose you?

THUMPER: (*Battle music grows louder*) Ah, dreams are a
funny thing. One day, your dream is to eat a world
record bowl of puddin', and the next day it is to
lead an army of spoon-wielding, true red Puddin'
Heads into battle against the dreaded Sweeties. In
your case, is not your dream to storm the castle, to
establish yourselves as the rightful ruling party, and
to cut down trees until you find the long-lost great
pot o' gold?

AXESTORM: It is!

SAWDUNCE: I don't know if all that is necessary to
reach our dreams. What if we're thwarted again?
Me wee hands can't take another round of
scraping!

AXESTORM: You heard the plan—your wee hands
won't be scraped!

SAWDUNCE: What about the catapult? How will I land?

AXESTORM: (*pulls off hat*) Parachutes!

THUMPER: (*music swelling*) Your dreams will not be fulfilled with an easy stroll down cupcake road—

SAWDUNCE: I like cupcakes. A lot of leprechauns like—

THUMPER: No! That road is strewn with traps set by the Sweeties, who lie in the ditches, waiting to ambush you with cake and cookies.

SAWDUNCE: I could really use a cookie right now.

THUMPER: No! You must sacrifice to make your dreams come true. You must take back what is yours! You need a glorious leader to light the true path to your glorious dreams. Will not finding the great pot o' gold make your dreams come true?!

AXESTORM: It will!

CHOPWIT: But how do we know your plan will work? The stakes couldn't be higher!

SAWDUNCE: If only the vast cosmos would give us a sign if Thumper should be our next leader.

THUMPER: You want a sign?! I'll give you a sign! (*pulls one large spoon from his spoon belt, banging it on his spoon helmet to the music*) Are there not spoons underneath your seats? (*pulls out the other large spoon from his spoon belt, now rapidly whacking both spoons on his spoon helmet to the beat, encouraging the judges and audience to do the same, who all have spoons underneath their chairs*)

The judges pull out two large spoons underneath their chairs, holding them up with amazement.

CHOPWIT: (*waving his spoons to the music, with an*

occasional whack to the noggin) What the—How is this possible?! Is this a magical sign from the universe? Or wait—(*to Axestorm*)—did you plant these spoons ahead of time? Have you been acting this whole time? Did you plan this all along?!

AXESTORM: (*whacking his head with spoons to the music, experimenting with covering his eyes*) What? That is ridiculous. I would never—you know I don't have the capacity to plan that far in advance. Isn't this moment the only sign that we need?

CHOPWIT: It is a sign of something.

SAWDUNCE: (*tests whacking his head*) Ow. It is a sign of something all right.

AXESTORM: (*to audience*) Oh, universe, if you have a sign, deliver it to us now. (*thunderclaps are nearby*) There are only two true choices. Should we choose ourselves as the next golden leaders? Or should Thumper become the next leader of the Lumberjack Leprechauns? (*waits for audience response, pacing*) Great awe-inspiring universe, as we weigh this difficult decision, tell us who we should choose as our new leader!

Audience members shout their choices. The judges huddle for several moments to reach their decision seemingly based on audience input.

AXESTORM: (*to audience*) After a day of witnessing candidates with special talents, based on messages that we received from the universe—some of which we may have ignored—and upon careful deliberation of this momentous decision, we have made a very difficult choice. We have selected Thumper as the next leader of the Lumberjack

Leprechauns!

THUMPER: Yes! Oh, glorious universe, your infinite wisdom will launch us into the stratosphere of truth once more!

AXESTORM: Yes! With the force of the universe, we will storm the castle by catapult! The second time's a charm.

CHOPWIT: Yes, this time we will charge with spoons!

SAWDUNCE: And green goggles!

THUMPER: And spoon helmets!

SAWDUNCE: And wee hat parachutes!

AXESTORM: And then all our dreams will come true!

Lightening flashes. Thunder crackles. Dramatic light shift.

New Scene

NARRATOR VOICE: A week later...

CHOPWIT: Ah, how the stars twinkle tonight.

SAWDUNCE: I was doubting this plan, but the stars are waving to us!

THUMPER. The weather is perfect for charging with spoons.

AXESTORM: These signs from the universe couldn't be clearer.

CHOPWIT: But I can't see anything in front of me.

SAWDUNCE: Turn on your green goggle night vision!

CHOPWIT: Oh. There we go!

THUMPER: Strap on your spoon helmets! Are you ready to catapult?

SAWDUNCE: Ready.

CHOPWIT: Ready.

AXESTORM: I've been waiting me whole life for this

moment. Ready!

THUMPER: Lumberjack Leprechauns... CHARGE!!!

Battle cries and "sheep" charging into battle are heard in the background. AXESTORM, CHOPWIT, SAWDUNCE, and THUMPER "fly" from catapults into the air.

Note: Get creative here with lighting, shadow play, physical theatre, puppets, or comedic imagination.

SAWDUNCE: I'm flying!

THUMPER: Steady. Steady!

SAWDUNCE: Oh no, I dropped me wee hat!

THUMPER: Look down there! Lumberjack Leprechauns are catapulting across the moat!

CHOPWIT: Gah! Some smashed against the castle wall!

THUMPER: There is no victory without sacrifice. Now look—50 leprechauns are stacked on top of each other, wearing spoon helmets, ready to head butt the castle door, with my very specialized training. They'll knock down the door the same time we land inside the castle!

CHOPWIT: Oh! They head butted too soon.

AXESTORM: Ugh!

SAWDUNCE: Ahh! They knocked themselves unconscious!

CHOPWIT: Wait a minute. We're flying too high!

AXESTORM: We're flying *over* the castle!

THUMPER: We got this! Ready your spoons!

SAWDUNCE: I'm still flying! Ahh! How am I going to land?

AXESTORM: Hang on to me. Everyone, use your parachutes! Watch out for the trees!

Dramatic light shift. AXESTORM, CHOPWIT, SAWDUNCE, and THUMPER collide with trees. Lights up. Everyone is collapsed and scattered across the battlefield.

CHOPWIT: (*moaning in pain*) Ow, my head. What were we thinking?!

SAWDUNCE: We failed *again*. But this time, I can barely move me wee arms!

AXESTORM: Oh, it hurts. Me whole body hurts. How am I going to chop trees? Or build things?

SAWDUNCE: But your parachute.

AXESTORM: It didn't work. Thumper, you shot us over the castle!

THUMPER: You can never have too much power.

AXESTORM: How is this possible? I was so certain.

CHOPWIT: Maybe we should have made a different choice?

SAWDUNCE: Yeah. Imagine that ending.

Light shift takes us back in time. AXESTORM, CHOPWIT, SAWDUNCE, and THUMPER return to their original places at the beginning of the scene for a different ending. Lights up.

AXESTORM: (*to audience*) After a day of witnessing candidates with special talent, based on messages that we received from the universe—some of which we may have ignored—and upon careful deliberation of this momentous decision, we have made a very difficult choice. We have selected Ourselves as the next leaders of the Lumberjack Leprechauns!

THUMPER: Aw, c'mon! What about restoring the monarchy?

CHOPWIT: We will give democracy a chance! And I will build an amazing pub to serve me lucky golden brew.

SAWDUNCE: And I will run for mayor to build a stronger community.

AXESTORM: And I will help build your dreams.

SAWDUNCE: And I will plant thousands of trees.

AXESTORM: Sawdunce!

SAWDUNCE: That's future Mayor Sawblade. With me open mind, I can see that planting trees is a good idea, even if it came from a Tree Hugger. There's a time for chopping trees. And a time for planting them.

AXESTORM: The fastest growing sapling will reveal the great buried pot o' gold!

THUMPER: What are you talking about? (*pulling spoons from backpack*) What am I going to do now? What am I supposed to do with all these spoons?!

SAWDUNCE: Wait! We can start a new golden tradition. A golden parade led by us! A parade where everyone is invited. We'll hand out cookies —

THUMPER: No!

SAWDUNCE: And tree samplings to plant.

AXESTORM: Can't wait to find that gold!

SAWDUNCE: And lucky golden brew.

CHOPWIT: Yes! But you need a golden crown to lead the parade.

SAWDUNCE: That would be nice. But we have spoons! (*holds up a spoon*)

Lightening flashes. Thunder crackles.

CHOPWIT: Uh, let's wait for the storm to pass.

NARRATOR VOICE: Minutes later.

SAWDUNCE: Spoons up! Let our golden journey begin!

Music plays. SAWDUNCE leads his crew through the aisles, encouraging audience members to march along and wave spoons. Eventually, SAWDUNCE and his crew return to the stage.

New scene. Light shift takes us back to the present. They are back in their same positions, scattered across the battlefield.

CHOPWIT: (*moaning in pain*) Yeah, that ending would have a slightly different outcome.

SAWDUNCE: Maybe it's not too late—

Suddenly, the KING appears, wearing a golden crown and carrying a pot o' gold.

KING: Loyal royal subjects, what are you doing?

AXESTORM: Your majesty!

KING: You charge *inside* the castle, not *outside* the castle!

AXESTORM: We missed.

KING: You missed the castle?! (*beat*) Are you... holding spoons? Why are you dressed like clowns wearing pan hats?

THUMPER: They are spoon helmets! (*to AXESTORM*) This sap is your king?

KING: What did you call me? Why are none of you bowing?

SAWDUNCE: It's difficult to move your majesty. We are badly injured attempting to storm the castle. Perhaps you could help us—

KING: Just like Stumpsharp. I don't reward attempts. I reward results! You call this loyalty?

CHOPWIT: (*dramatic shift*) Are you for real? Do you know what we have sacrificed? For you?

KING: How am I going to regain power from the leafnuts?!

CHOPWIT: A better question is, How are we going to make our dreams come true?

KING: Your dreams will never come true without the great pot o' gold.

CHOPWIT: I don't think there is great pot o' gold.

SAWDUNCE: I don't think the stars were waving at us.

KING: Have the leafnuts confused your mind? Finding the great pot o' gold has been your mission for generations! Because once you actually storm the castle, I will return to power, you can continue chopping trees until all have fallen, and finally, at long last, fulfill your mission.

CHOPWIT: No, you are confused. It is the monarchy that has fallen.

AXESTORM: Chopwit, stop thinking! I'm sorry. I got it wrong. It's the *third* time that's the charm!

THUMPER: Indeed. Next time, we will prove victorious. I am certain of it!

SAWDUNCE: You said that last time. Perhaps we should lead ourselves.

CHOPWIT: Perhaps it isn't too late.

KING: You'll do as I command!

CHOPWIT: Sorry, I'm no longer taking orders from royal deadwood.

SAWDUNCE: (*laughs*) He's only taking orders for his lucky golden brew!

CHOPWIT: (*laughs*) Bahhh!

SAWDUNCE: And we'll take a golden crown for payment. (*attempts to take the KING's crown, the KING scurries away, CHOPWIT chases the KING and eventually grabs the crown*) It's time for a new leader, with a mind of gold! (*places the crown on CHOPWIT*)

KING: The crown is not something to joke about! It belongs to me!

CHOPWIT: No, no. The crown belongs to a leader with a heart of gold. I insist. (*places crown on SAWDUNCE*)

SAWDUNCE: Now I *can* lead a golden parade. (*SAWDUNCE and CHOPWIT cheerily parade around, avoiding the KING*)

KING: Give me back my crown! Where are my loyal followers?

THUMPER: (*struggles in pain to strap spoon helmet on the KING's head*) Perfect fit. You can join me.

KING: (*holding up gold coins*) You're working for me!

CHOPWIT: No. This belongs to the people now. (*pulls away the pot o' gold. SAWDUNCE cheers*)

KING: You've all gone mad!

AXESTORM: I haven't your highness. Chopwit, Sawdunce, the third time will be a charm, I swear it! (*tries but fails to take the pot o' gold from CHOPWIT*)

CHOPWIT: After our injuries, how is your mind as dull as a battered axe? Can you not see this royal shenanigan?

AXESTORM: Long live the king!

AXESTORM, THUMPER, and the KING chase

CHOPWIT with the pot o' gold and SAWDUNCE
with the golden crown, trying to take them away. They
chase each other in circles, pulling the crown and gold back
and forth, perhaps spilling gold. The chaos continues in the
background, shifts to slow motion, or freezes. CHOPWIT
blocks others from reaching SAWDUNCE and the
crown. Spotlight on SAWDUNCE who places the crown
on a table, grabs his axe, and paces beside it.

SAWDUNCE:

Lumberjack Leprechauns, torn in their stance,
Guided by cosmic wisdom's dance?
They catapulted to restore,
Their king's power and more,
But the trees set them back with a glance.

As stars watched over their plight,
Their rift grew deep by moonlight,
The universe watched, quite amused,
For what future would they choose,
With golden loyalty split that night?
(SAWDUNCE raises his axe to chop the crown.)

Lights fade to black.

Dear Reader,

Thanks for reading *The Golden One*. If you enjoyed this play, please consider taking a few seconds to provide a rating or a minute or two to leave an honest review on your favorite store. Reviews make a big difference in connecting readers with new authors and works. Thank you for your time and support!

Sincerely,

W.T. Kosmos

W.T. KOSMOS

wtkosmos.com

W.T. Kosmos is the humorist author of the award-winning *Blaze Union and the Puddin' Head Schools* and the *Maya and Waggers* series. He is the alter ego (pen name) of a life-long educator who has had the great privilege and joy of serving as a teacher and school principal. W.T. Kosmos lives along the coast of Paradox, USA, Earth, Milky Way and enjoys reading, writing, walking the beach, star gazing, snorkeling with Regal the seahorse, and wrestling with his magnificent dogs. He is also an aspiring professional wrestler.

𝕏 wtkosmos

f wtkauthor

⊙ wtkosmos

Made in the USA
Monee, IL
08 June 2024

59523674R00049